THE
ELEMENTS OF STYLE

By William Strunk Jr.

CLASSIC EDITION

UPDATED & EDITED
By Richard De A'Morelli

SPECTRUM INK PUBLISHING
"Tomorrow's Great Classics Today"

The Elements of Style: Classic Edition

ISBN numbers:

978-1-988236-51-3	Paperback
978-1-988236-50-6	Mobi
978-1-988236-49-0	Epub
978-1-988236-48-3	Paperback (large print)

Spectrum Ink Canada
Vancouver, British Columbia

Spectrum Ink USA
San Luis Obispo, California

Online:
http://vu.org/books

Table of Contents

Foreword

GRAMMAR AND STYLE FOR THE 21ˢᵗ CENTURY

Excerpted from *Elements of Style 2017*, by Richard De A'Morelli
— https://amazon.com/dp/B01MD0396I

Years ago, when my first magazine article was published shortly after my fourteenth birthday and I set my heart on writing as my life's ambition, there weren't many resources available for aspiring writers. Amazon.com was decades off in the future. We purchased paperbacks from the local bookstore, subscribed to *Writer's Digest* magazine, and borrowed a handful of books from the public library. I owned several dictionaries, a thesaurus, some paperbacks on writing and vocabulary, a high school grammar text-book, and a thin book with a cloth cover and faded pages: *The Elements of Style*. It was an indispensable reference that I reached for often when writing and editing my early books and articles.

The Elements of Style was written one hundred years ago by William Strunk Jr., an English professor at Cornell University. Over the years, generations of college students and writers have learned the basics of grammar from this short handbook. It was rated "one of the 100 most influential books written in English" by *Time* in 2011, and iconic author Stephen King recommends it as a grammar hand-book that all aspiring writers should read.

This Classic Edition is meant as a tribute to Prof. Strunk's book that has endured down through the years. Many of the grammar rules it mentions are as valid today as they were a century ago; but, one by one, these rules have grown out-of-date. Another shortcoming of the book is that it does not include essential grammar and style rules today's writers should know in this era of technology and self-publishing.

Last summer, I set out to update Prof. Strunk's book. I had intended to delete obsolete rules and add new rules which are widely followed today. As I worked through the project, I kept thinking: "Wait, maybe I should add this...and this... and this." As the weeks passed, my "quick update" grew into 250 pages packed with updated grammar and style rules. I drew from a variety of sources besides Strunk's book, and I eventually finished the project, which is now available on Amazon. Com as *Elements of Style 2017.*

But I had not accomplished my original goal: to produce a tribute edition of Strunk's original book, with footnotes calling attention to grammar rules that no longer apply in the present day. So I circled back for another try, and this book is the end result.

Before we delve into Chapter 1, let's review briefly what grammar is, and why it matters so much in today's world. Simply put, grammar is concerned with how words are used and put together to form sentences and paragraphs. Style refers to an additional set of rules many writers, and all professional editors, follow to edit and proofread book manuscripts and other documents. A knowledge of grammar is important because it will help you to write sentences that make sense. Style rules are just as important because they will help you to turn a first draft into a publication-ready, final draft manuscript.

Style rules cover a wide range of issues, above and beyond the basic principles of grammar, from questions on word usage to capitalization, punctuation, how to abbreviate, and how to write numbers. Style rules fill in the gray areas that exist because some grammar rules tend to be broad. For example, *Chicago Manual of Style*, the world's most widely referenced style guide, advises that numbers up to one hundred must be spelled out, and values over that should be written as digits. Thus we would write: *The alphabet has twenty-six letters, and a year has 365 days.*

Let's take a look at what can happen when we stray from consistent adherence to basic style rules:

> Nine men stood by the wall, and 4 women stood next to the 2 cars. When the police approached the 9 men, they scattered, and the four women jumped into the two cars and sped away.

This hodgepodge of digits and spelled-out numbers makes the paragraph seem badly written. Inconsistent style disrupts the flow of a manuscript, making it difficult for readers to follow. Diligently adhering to a set of style rules from start to finish will result in a cleanly edited manuscript that reads well, and one that the writer can hand in at work or school, submit to an agent or publisher, or self-publish with a reasonable expectation of positive reviews and sales.

In online writing groups and at social gatherings, some writers can be heard arguing that grammar and style don't matter—it's the story that counts! In fact, that's not the case. Surveys have shown that book buyers expect published works to be cleanly edited and free of typos. Badly edited books—and unfortunately, many self-published books fall under that heading—typically see few or no sales and receive harsh reviews from readers who know good writing from bad and don't mind saying so.

Numerous writing style guides are used today, of which *Elements of Style* is one. The most authoritative style guides are: *Chicago Manual of Style*, the bible of editors working in American English fiction genres, and some nonfiction editors; *AP Stylebook*, used by journalists and many others who write and edit for news organizations and websites; and *APA Style,* used mostly by college students for writing term papers and essays. In the United Kingdom, *Oxford Style Guide* is widely followed. Many other style guides are used in government, academia, and by niche publishers.

Modern style guides are packed with often complicated rules on grammar, punctuation, and other relevant issues. A working editor might have devoted months or years to learning these rules. This investment of time and the level of skill required to do a good job of editing presents a high bar for writers who want to self-edit and submit a manuscript to a publisher with the imprimatur of being cleanly edited and proofread, and for those who wish to self-publish but cannot afford to hire an experienced editor.

Style guides sometimes offer conflicting advice, creating confusion among writers and even editors. *Elements of Style* will tell you to write one way; *Chicago Manual of Style,* or CMoS, may tell you to do the opposite! As one example, CMoS mandates the use of serial commas, while *AP Stylebook* advises against them. So if you are editing to AP Style and use a serial comma, it's an error; if you follow Chicago Style and don't use a serial comma, that's an error. Many novice writers don't even know what a serial comma is! It's not well defined in *Elements of Style*, so I inserted a brief notation to explain it in this updated version.

Strunk's grammar book stresses the importance of writing concise, grammatically correct prose. It reminds us that the writer's objective is to communicate with words, to inform or entertain readers by imparting information in an efficient and eloquent manner. The clearer one's writing is, the more likely readers will understand the points being made.

Good writing is built on patterns of words and sentences, so whether you are writing a news story, a press release, a spicy love story, or a memoir, you must be consistent with your style. Don't refer to an iPhone in one paragraph and then call it a cell phone in the next, and a mobile device on the following page. Switching back and forth from one style to another does not add interest to your prose—it confuses readers and muddles the points you've set out to make. Avoid using different numbering schemes, for example, in which you write *10 pens* in one sentence and *ten pens* in the next. Readers will notice and be distracted by these variations. Be consistent with punctuation too. If you start out using serial commas in your manuscript, use them throughout so that every sentence is consistently punctuated rather than written in a haphazard fashion.

Prof. Strunk refers to "points of view" in his book, but the term is not well explained. No doubt he assumed that readers learned these grammar basics in early school years; and you probably did; but whether you remember them years later is another matter. So for the sake of clarity, let's take a moment to revisit points of view in writing.

First person is when the person is speaking. Stories written from this point of view make use of first-person forms of personal pronouns (*I, we, me, us, my, our, mine,* and *ours*).

> I spent the summer touring the mountains of Oregon and Washington. **My brother and I** shared the driving, and **we** camped out under the stars.

This voice is used in autobiographies and memoirs. It is occasionally used in fiction writing; but writing stories in first person is difficult and requires a decent measure of skill. Many writers don't handle first-person point of view particularly well.

Second person represents a person or thing spoken to. This voice is sometimes used in nonfiction writing, especially in the self-help, how-to, and do-it-yourself genres. It is rarely used in fiction. Second-person pronouns include *you, your,* and *yours.*

> For a summer adventure, **you** can tour the mountains of Oregon and Washington. If **you** travel with a companion, **you** can share the driving and save money by camping out under the stars.

Third person is when the character, event, or object is spoken about. This is the voice most often used for writing news and other nonfiction, and for most fiction. Third-person pronouns include: *he, him, his, she, her, hers, they, them, their, theirs, it,* and *its.*

> Charles spent the summer touring the mountains of Oregon and Washington. **He** shared the driving with **his brother** and camped out under the stars.

Choosing the appropriate voice for a book or other project will depend to a large extent upon the project itself and your target audience. Once you have decided on a point of view, stay with it and don't shift from one voice to another. If you decide to write in third person, maintain that point of view throughout your manuscript.

The point of view you decide to write from can make or break a project, so it's a crucial choice. The short paragraph below is written in second person (you). As you will see, this voice can be confusing for readers and difficult to follow when the word *you* is used as a general pronoun.

> Most commercially available electricity is generated by turbines that convert steam into electricity. **You can produce steam in several ways.**

The writer's approach is awkward and irrelevant to readers who are not involved in a utility business that produces steam for power-generating turbines. But with a few quick edits, the voice can be changed to third person:

> Most commercially available electricity is generated by turbines that convert steam into electricity. **Steam can be produced in several ways.**

Notice how changing the voice improves the flow of the passage, and further, how removing the general pronoun "you" gives it a more authoritative tone.

With these grammar pointers in mind, let's move on to Prof. Strunk's *Elements of Style*. The original version follows in these next pages with a few enhancements:

1. Editorial notes (clearly labeled) have been inserted to indicate obsolete grammar rules, and to brief provide insights on updated rules for contemporary writers.

2. Easily recognizable symbols have been added to the grammar examples throughout the book so that readers can discern correctly written sentences from errors at a glance.

3. A brief Study Guide has been added at the conclusion of the book.

4. The paperback version of this Classic Edition includes blank, lined pages at the end for convenient note taking.

5. The digital version has been restyled for improved display on the latest generation of Kindle devices and other e-book readers.

Prof. Strunk's book is a nostalgic reminder of a momentous time in American history that ushered in the Art Deco era and the Roaring Twenties. But our world has changed, and the rules of English grammar and style have changed with it. For a complete handbook of nearly 500 up-to-date grammar and style rules, please consider *Elements of Style 2017*, available in Kindle and paperback editions at https://amazon.com/dp/B01MD0396I

Thank you for taking the time to read this short book, and good luck with your writing projects!

Richard De A'Morelli
Editor

Chapter 1

INTRODUCTORY

This book aims to describe in just a few pages the principal requirements of plain English style. Its goal is to lighten the task of instructors and students by concentrating on a few essentials (particularly in Chapters 2 and 3), the rules of usage, and principles of composition most commonly violated. To fulfill these criteria, the book will describe three rules for the use of the comma, rather than a dozen or more, and one for the use of the semicolon, in the belief that these four rules will provide for most of the punctuation that is required by nineteen sentences out of twenty. Likewise, the book discusses in Chapter 3 only those principles pertaining to the paragraph and the sentence which are of the widest application. Thus, we will endeavor to cover only a small portion of the field of English grammar and style. This writer's experience has shown that once students have mastered these essentials, they will profit most by individual instruction based on the problems of their own work, and that each instructor has his own body of theories on grammar, which he may prefer to that offered by any textbook.

The writer's colleagues in the Department of English at Cornell University have greatly helped him in preparing this manuscript. Mr. George McLane Wood has kindly consented to inclusion under Rule 10 of selected material from his *Suggestions to Authors*.

The following books on grammar and writing are recommended for reference or further study: in connection with Chapters 2 and 4, F. Howard Collins, *Author and Printer* (Henry Frowde); Chicago University Press, *Manual of Style*; T. L. De Vinne, *Correct Composition* (The Century Co.); Horace Hart, *Rules for Compositors and Printers* (Oxford University Press); George McLane Wood, *Extracts from the Style-Book of the Government Printing Office* (United States Geological Survey); in connection with Chapters 3 and 5, *The King's English* (Oxford University Press); Sir Arthur Quiller-Couch, *The Art of Writing* (Putnam), especially the chapter, "Interlude on Jargon"; George McLane Wood, *Suggestions to Authors* (United States Geological Survey); John Lesslie Hall, *English Usage* (Scott, Foresman & Co.); James P. Kelley, *Workmanship in Words* (Little, Brown and Co.). In these will be found full discussions of many points covered briefly in this writing style guide.

It is an old observation that the best writers sometimes disregard the rules of rhetoric. When they do so, however, readers will usually find in the sentence some compensating merit to counterbalance the cost of the violation. Unless a writer is certain that he will provide the same benefit, he will probably do best to follow the rules. After the writer has learned, by studying and adhering to the rules, to write plain English adequate for everyday use, let him look for the secrets of style in studying the masters of literature.

Chapter 2

ELEMENTARY RULES OF USAGE

Rule 1. Form the possessive singular of nouns by adding 's.

Follow this rule regardless of the final consonant. These usages are correct:

Charles's friend

Burns's poems

the witch's malice

This is the rule followed by the U.S. Government Printing Office and the Oxford University Press.

Exceptions are the possessive of ancient proper names ending in -es and -is; the possessive *Jesus'*; and such forms as *for conscience' sake, for righteousness' sake.* But such forms as Achilles' *heel, Moses' laws, Isis' temple* are commonly rewritten as:

the heel of Achilles

the laws of Moses

the temple of Isis

Do not use an apostrophe with the pronominal possessives *hers, its, theirs, yours,* and *oneself.*

Rule 2. In a series of three or more terms with a single conjunction, use a comma after each term except the last.

For example:

> red, white, and blue
>
> gold, silver, or copper
>
> He opened the letter, read it, and made a note of its contents.

This is consistent with the guidelines of the Government Printing Office and of the Oxford University Press.

[*Editor's Note:* A comma placed before a conjunction in a series of three or more terms is called a serial comma or an Oxford comma. Depending on the particular style guide the writer is using, such commas either may be required or proscribed in present-day writing. *Chicago Manual of Style*, for instance, states that serial commas should be used, while Associated Press Stylebook cautions against them. For details on serial commas in modern usage, refer to Chapter 12 in *Elements of Style 2017*.]

In the names of business firms omit the last comma, as,

> Brown, Shipley & Co.

Rule 3. Enclose parenthetic expressions between commas.

A parenthetic expression is a clause or phrase that is inserted within another clause or phrase. In a sense, it interrupts the flow of the first expression; usually, it can be omitted and you will still have a complete sentence, as,

> The best way to see a country, unless you are
> pressed for time, is to travel on foot.

This rule is difficult to apply, as it is often hard to decide whether a single word, such as *however*, or a brief phrase, is or is not parenthetic. If the interruption to the flow of the sentence is but slight, the writer may safely omit the commas. But whether the interruption be slight or considerable, one comma must be never inserted and the other omitted. In the following examples, only a single comma is used, and none of these expressions are correct:

> ✗ Marjorie's husband, Colonel Nelson paid us a visit yesterday.

> ✗ My brother you will be pleased to hear, is now in perfect health.

If a parenthetic expression is preceded by a conjunction, write the first comma before the conjunction, not after it.

> ☺ He saw us coming, and unaware that we had learned of his treachery, greeted us with a smile.

The following constructions should always be regarded as parenthetic expressions and should be enclosed between commas (or, at the end of the sentence, between a comma and a period):

1. the year, when forming part of a date, and the day of the month, when following the day of the week:

> February to July, 1916

> April 6, 1917

> Monday, November 11, 1918

2. the abbreviations *etc.* and *jr.*

3. non-restrictive relative clauses, meaning those which do not serve to identify or define the antecedent noun, and similar clauses introduced by conjunctions indicating time or place.

> ✗ The audience, which had at first been indifferent, became more and more interested.

In the above sentence, the clause introduced by *which* does not clearly identify which of several possible audiences is being referenced; what audience is in question is supposed to be already known. The clause adds, parenthetically, a statement supplementing that in the main clause. The sentence is virtually a combination of two statements which could have been written independently:

> ☺ The audience had at first been indifferent. It became more and more interested.

Compare the restrictive relative clause, not set off by commas, in this sentence:

> ☺ The candidate who best meets these requirements will be hired for the job.

Here the clause introduced by *who* does serve to tell which of several possible candidates is meant; the sentence cannot be split up into two independent statements.

The difference in punctuation in the two sentences following is based on the same principle:

> Nether Stowey, where Coleridge wrote *The Rime of the Ancient Mariner*, is just a few miles from Bridgewater.

> The day will come when you will admit your mistake.

Nether Stowey is completely identified by its name; the statement about Coleridge is therefore supplementary and parenthetic. The *day* spoken of is identified only by the dependent clause, which is therefore restrictive.

Similar in principle to the enclosing of parenthetic expressions between commas is the setting off by commas of phrases or dependent clauses preceding or following the main clause of a sentence. For example:

> Partly by hard fighting, partly by diplomatic skill, they enlarged their dominions to the east, and rose to royal rank with the possession of Sicily, exchanged afterwards for Sardinia.

Other illustrations may be found in sentences quoted under Rules 4, 5, 6, 7, 16 and 18 below.

Be careful that you do not set off independent clauses by commas. See Rule 5 for clarification and examples.

Rule 4. Place a comma before a conjunction introducing a co-ordinate clause.

> ✗ The early records of the city have disappeared, and the story of its first years can no longer be reconstructed.

> ✗ The situation is perilous, but there is still one chance of escape.

Sentences of this type, isolated from their context, may seem to be in need of rewriting. They make sense when we reach the comma, and the second clause has the appearance of an afterthought. Further, the conjunction *and* is the least specific of connectives. Used between independent clauses, it indicates only that a relation exists between them without defining that relation. In the example above, the relation is that of cause and result. The two sentences might be rewritten:

> ☺ As the early records of the city have disappeared, the story of its first years can no longer be reconstructed.

> ☺ Although the situation is perilous, there is still one chance of escape.

Or the subordinate clauses might be replaced by phrases:

> ☺ Owing to the disappearance of the early records of the city, the story of its first years can no longer be reconstructed.

> ☺ In this perilous situation, there is still one chance of escape.

It is not necessarily good style to make all of your sentences too uniformly compact and periodic. An occasional loose sentence prevents the style from becoming too formal and gives the reader a bit of relief. Consequently, loose sentences of the type first quoted are common in casual, non-technical writing. But be careful not to construct too many of your sentences after this pattern (see Rule 14).

Two-part sentences of which the second member is introduced by *as* (in the sense of *because*), *for, or, nor,* and *while* (in the sense of *and at the same time*) likewise require a comma before the conjunction.

If the second member is introduced by an adverb, a semi-colon rather than a comma is required (see Rule 5). The connectives *so* and *yet* may be used either as adverbs or as conjunctions, accordingly as the second clause is felt to be co-ordinate or subordinate; so either punctuation mark may be appropriate. Note, however, that these uses of *so* (equivalent to *accordingly* or to *so that*) are somewhat colloquial and should, as a rule, be avoided in writing. A simple correction that usually works is to omit the word *so* and begin the first clause with *as* or *since*:

☺ As I had never been in the place before, I had difficulty in finding my way about.

This construction is preferable to:

✗ I had never been in the place before; so I had difficulty in finding my way about.

If a dependent clause, or an introductory phrase that must be set off by a comma, precedes the second independent clause, no comma is needed after the conjunction.

☺ The situation is perilous, but if we are prepared to act promptly, there is still one chance of escape.

When the subject is the same for both clauses and is expressed only once, a comma is required if the connective is *but*. If the connective is *and*, omit the comma if the relation between the two statements is close or immediate.

☺ I have heard his arguments, but am still unconvinced.

☺ He has had several years' experience and is thoroughly competent.

Rule 5. Do not join independent clauses by a comma.

If two or more clauses, grammatically complete and not joined by a conjunction, are written to form a compound sentence, the proper punctuation mark is a semicolon.

☺ Stevenson's romances are entertaining; they are full of exciting adventures.

☺ It is nearly half past five; we cannot reach town before dark.

It is equally correct to write the above as two sentences each and replace the semicolons by periods.

☺ Stevenson's romances are entertaining. They are full of exciting adventures.

☺ It is nearly half past five. We cannot reach town before dark.

If a conjunction is inserted the proper mark is a comma (Rule 4).

☺ Stevenson's romances are entertaining, for they are full of exciting adventures.

☺ It is nearly half past five, and we cannot reach town before dark.

A comparison of the three forms given above will show clearly that the first is preferable. It is, at least in the examples given, better than the second form, because it suggests the close relationship between the two statements in a way that the second does not attempt. It is better than the third, because it is briefer and therefore more direct and concise. Indeed, this simple method of indicating relationship between statements is one of the most useful devices of composition. The relationship, as in the above examples, is commonly one of cause or of consequence.

Note that if the second clause is preceded by an adverb, such as *accordingly, besides, then, therefore,* or *thus,* and not by a conjunction, the semicolon is still required.

But note two exceptions to this rule. First, if the clauses are very short and are alike in form, a comma is usually acceptable:

☺ Man proposes, God disposes.

☺ The gate swung apart, the bridge fell, the portcullis was drawn up.

Note that in these examples the relation is not one of cause or consequence. Also in the colloquial form of expression, as the following, a comma, not a semicolon, is required:

☺ I hardly knew him, he was so changed,

However, this form of expression is not appropriate in writing, except in the dialogue of a story or play, or perhaps in a familiar letter or other casual writing.

Rule 6. Do not break sentences in two.

In other words, do not use periods for commas. While it is acceptable to break a compound sentence into two shorter elements, where both form complete sentences, but doing so often results in choppy wording. Especially avoid breaking sentences in two when one part or the other does not form a complete sentence, as,

✘ I met them on a Cunard liner several years ago. Coming home from Liverpool to New York.

✘ He was an interesting talker. A man who had traveled all over the world and lived in half a dozen countries.

In both these examples, the first period should be replaced by a comma, and the following word written with a lower case letter.

It is permissible to make an emphatic word or expression serve the purpose of a sentence and to punctuate it accordingly:

☺ Again and again he called out. No reply.

You must be certain, however, that the emphasis is warranted, and that you will not be suspected of a mere blunder in syntax or in punctuation.

Rules 3, 4 5, and 6 cover the most important principles in the punctuation of ordinary sentences; they should be so thoroughly mastered that their application becomes second nature.

Rule 7. A participial phrase at the beginning of a sentence must refer to the grammatical subject.

Walking slowly down the road, he saw a woman accompanied by two children.

The word *walking* refers to the subject of the sentence, not to the woman. If you want to make it refer to the woman, you must recast the sentence:

He saw a woman accompanied by two children, walking slowly down the road.

Participial phrases preceded by a conjunction or preposition, nouns in apposition, adjectives, and adjective phrases come under the same rule if they begin the sentence.

✗ On arriving in Chicago, his friends met him at the station.

☺ When he arrived (or, On his arrival) in Chicago, his friends met him at the station.

✗ A soldier of proved valor, they entrusted him with the defense of the city.

☺ A soldier of proved valor, he was entrusted with the defense of the city.

✗ Young and inexperienced, the task seemed easy to me.

☺ Young and inexperienced, I thought the task easy.

✗ Without a friend to counsel him, the temptation proved irresistible.

☺ Without a friend to counsel him, he found the temptation irresistible.

Sentences violating this rule are often confusing and difficult for the reader to understand.

✗ Being in a dilapidated condition, I was able to buy the house very cheap.

✗ Wondering irresolutely what to do next, the clock struck twelve.

Chapter 3

ELEMENTARY PRINCIPLES OF COMPOSITION

Rule 8. Make the paragraph the unit of composition.

Write one paragraph to each topic. A paragraph expresses a complete thought.

If the subject on which you are writing is of a trivial nature, or if you intend to treat it very briefly, there may be no need to subdivide it into topics. Thus a brief description, a brief book review or summary of a new story, a brief account of a single incident, a narrative that merely outlines an action, the expressing of a single idea, any one of these is best written in a single paragraph. After the paragraph has been written, examine it to see whether you can improve the clarity by subdividing it.

In most other cases, however, a subject should be subdivided into topics, and each topic should be made the subject of a paragraph. The point of doing this is, of course, to aid the reader. The beginning of each paragraph is a signal to the reader that a new step in the development of the subject has been reached.

The extent of subdivision required will vary with the length of the composition. For example, a short notice of a book or poem might consist of a single paragraph. One slightly longer might consist of two paragraphs:

First paragraph: account of the work

Second paragraph: critical discussion

A report on a poem, written for a literature class, might consist of seven paragraphs:

1. Facts of composition and publication

2. Kind of poem; metrical form

3. Subject

4. Treatment of subject

5. For what chiefly remarkable

6. Wherein characteristic of the writer

7. Relationship to other works

The contents of paragraphs 3 and 4 would vary with the poem. Usually, paragraph 3 would indicate the actual or imagined circumstances of the poem (the situation), if these call for explanation, and would then state the subject and outline its development. If the poem is a narrative in the third person throughout, paragraph 3 need contain no more than a concise summary of the action. Paragraph 4 would indicate the leading ideas and show how they are made prominent, or would indicate what points in the narrative are mainly emphasized.

A novel might be discussed under the heads:

1. Setting

2. Plot

3. Characters

4. Purpose

An historical event might be discussed under the heads:

1. What led up to the event

2. Account of the event

3. What the event led up to

In treating either of these last two subjects, you would probably find it necessary to subdivide one or more of the suggested topics.

Generally speaking, single sentences should not be written or printed as paragraphs. One exception may be made in sentences of transition, indicating the relation between the parts of an exposition or argument. Frequent exceptions are also necessary in textbooks, guidebooks, and other works in which many topics are treated briefly.

In dialogue, each speech, even if only a single word, is a paragraph by itself. In other words, a new paragraph begins with each change of speaker. The application of this rule, when dialogue and narrative are combined, is best learned by studying examples in well-written works of fiction.

Rule 9. Begin each paragraph with a topic sentence.

Begin each paragraph with a topic sentence and end it in conformity with the beginning, although certain exceptions apply. Again, the object is to help the reader gain clarity and understanding of what you are writing. The practice recommended here enables readers to discover the purpose of each paragraph as they begin to read it, and to retain this purpose in mind as they end it. For this reason, the most useful kind of paragraph, particularly in exposition and argument, is that in which:

(a) the topic sentence comes at or near the beginning;

(b) the succeeding sentences explain, establish, or develop the statement made in the topic sentence; and

(c) the final sentence either emphasizes the thought of the topic sentence or states some important consequence.

Avoid ending with a digression or an unimportant detail.

If the paragraph forms part of a larger composition, its relation to what precedes, or its function as a part of the whole, may need to be expressed. This can be done sometimes by a mere word or phrase (*again*; *therefore*; *for the same reason*) in the topic sentence. Other times, however, it is expedient to precede the topic sentence by one or more sentences of introduction or transition. If more than one such sentence is required, it is generally better to set apart the transitional sentences as a separate paragraph.

According to the message you are trying to communicate in your writing, you may, as indicated above, relate the body of the paragraph to the topic sentence in one or more of several different ways. You may make the meaning of the topic sentence clearer by restating it in other forms; by defining its terms; by denying the contrary; or by giving illustrations or specific instances. Similarly, you may establish it by proofs; or you may develop it by showing its implications and consequences. In a long paragraph, you may carry out several of these processes.

Consider the following:

> [1] Now, to be properly enjoyed, a walking tour should be gone upon alone. [2] If you go in a company, or even in pairs, it is no longer a walking tour in anything but name; it is something else and more in the nature of a picnic. [3] A walking tour should be gone upon alone, because freedom

is of the essence; because you should be able to stop and go on, and follow this way or that, as the freak takes you; and because you must have your own pace, and neither trot alongside a champion walker, nor mince in time with a girl. [4] And you must be open to all impressions and let your thoughts take color from what you see. [5] You should be as a pipe for any wind to play upon. [6] "I cannot see the wit," says Hazlitt, "of walking and talking at the same time. [7] When I am in the country, I wish to vegetate like the country," which is the gist of all that can be said upon the matter. [8] There should be no cackle of voices at your elbow, to jar on the meditative silence of the morning. [9] And so long as a man is reasoning he cannot surrender himself to that fine intoxication that comes of much motion in the open air, that begins in a sort of dazzle and sluggishness of the brain, and ends in a peace that passes comprehension.—Stevenson, *Walking Tours*.

Let's break down the sentences comprising this paragraph.

1. Topic sentence.

2. The meaning made clearer by denial of the contrary.

3. The topic sentence repeated, in abridged form, and supported by three reasons; the meaning of the third ("you must have your own pace") made clearer by denying the contrary.

4. A fourth reason, stated in two forms.

5. The same reason, stated in still another form.

6–7. The same reason as stated by Hazlitt.

8. Repetition, in paraphrase, of the quotation from Hazlitt.

9. Final statement of the fourth reason, in language amplified and heightened to form a strong conclusion.

Let's consider another example:

> [1] It was chiefly in the eighteenth century that a very different conception of history grew up. [2] Historians then came to believe that their task was not so much to paint a picture as to solve a problem; to explain or illustrate the successive phases of national growth, prosperity, and adversity. [3] The history of morals, of industry, of intellect, and of art; the changes that take place in manners or beliefs; the dominant ideas that prevailed in successive periods; the rise, fall, and modification of political constitutions; in a word, all the conditions of national well-being became the subject of their works. [4] They sought rather to write a history of peoples than a history of kings. [5] They looked especially in history for the chain of causes and effects. [6] They undertook to study in the past the physiology of nations, and hoped by applying the experimental method on a large scale to deduce some lessons of real value about the conditions on which the welfare of society mainly depend.—Lecky, *The Political Value of History.*

1. Topic sentence.

2. The meaning of the topic sentence made clearer; the new conception of history defined.

3. The definition expanded.

4. The definition explained by contrast.

5. The definition supplemented: another element in the new conception of history.

6. Conclusion: an important consequence of the new conception of history.

In narration and description, the paragraph sometimes begins with a concise, comprehensive statement serving to hold together the details that follow.

> The breeze served us admirably.

> The campaign opened with a series of reverses.

> The next ten or twelve pages were filled with a curious set of entries.

But this device, if too often used, can become a mannerism. More commonly the opening sentence simply indicates by its subject with what the paragraph is to be principally concerned.

> At length I thought I might return towards the stockade.

> He picked up the heavy lamp from the table and began to explore.

> Another flight of steps, and they emerged on the roof.

The brief paragraphs of animated narrative, however, are often without even this semblance of a topic sentence. The break between them serves the purpose of a rhetorical pause, throwing into prominence some detail of the action.

Rule 10. Use the active voice.

The active voice is usually more direct and vigorous than the passive:

> ☺ I shall always remember my first visit to Boston.

This is much better than:

> ✗ My first visit to Boston will always be remembered by me.

The latter sentence is less direct, less bold, and less concise. If the writer tries to make it more concise by omitting "by me,"

> ✗ My first visit to Boston will always be remembered,

it becomes indefinite: is it the writer, or some undisclosed person, or the world at large, that will always remember this visit?

This rule does not mean that the writer should entirely discard the passive voice, which is often convenient and sometimes necessary.

> ☺ The dramatists of the Restoration are little esteemed today.

> ☺ Modern readers have little esteem for the dramatists of the Restoration.

The first would be the right form in a paragraph on the dramatists of the Restoration; the second, in a paragraph on the tastes of modern readers. The need to make a particular word the subject of the sentence will often, as in these examples, determine which voice is appropriate to use.

As a rule, avoid making one passive depend directly upon another.

✗ Gold was not allowed to be exported.

☺ It was forbidden to export gold (The export of gold was prohibited).

✗ He has been proved to have been seen entering the building.

☺ It has been proved that he was seen to enter the building.

In both the examples above, before correction, the word properly related to the second passive is made the subject of the first.

A common fault is to use as the subject of a passive construction a noun that expresses the entire action, leaving to the verb no function other than completing the sentence.

✗ A survey of this region was made in 1900.

☺ This region was surveyed in 1900.

✗ Mobilization of the army was rapidly effected.

☺ The army was rapidly mobilized.

✗ Confirmation of these reports cannot be obtained.

☺ These reports cannot be confirmed.

Compare the sentence in the first set of examples, "The export of gold was prohibited," in which the predicate "was prohibited" expresses something not implied in "export."

The habitual use of the active voice makes for forcible writing. This is true not only in narrative mainly concerned with action, but in writing of any kind. Many bland descriptive sentences can be made lively and more emphatic by substituting a verb in the active voice for some such perfunctory expression as *there is*, or *could be heard*.

✗ There were a great number of dead leaves lying on the ground.

☺ Dead leaves covered the ground.

✗ The sound of a guitar somewhere in the house could be heard.

☺ Somewhere in the house a guitar hummed sleepily.

✗ The reason that he left college was that his health became impaired.

☺ Failing health compelled him to leave college.

✗ It was not long before he was very sorry that he had said what he had.

☺ He soon repented his words.

Rule 11. Put statements in positive form.

Make definite assertions in your writing. Avoid tame, colorless, hesitating, non-committal language. Use the word *not* as a means of denial or in antithesis, never as a means of evasion.

✗ He was not very often on time.

☺ He usually came late.

✗ He did not think that studying Latin was much use.

☺ He thought the study of Latin useless.

✗ *The Taming of the Shrew* is rather weak in spots. Shakespeare does not portray Katharine as a very admirable character, nor does Bianca remain long in memory as an important character in Shakespeare's works.

☺ The women in *The Taming of the Shrew* are unattractive. Katharine is disagreeable, Bianca insignificant.

The last example, before correction, is indefinite as well as negative. The corrected version, consequently, is merely a guess at the writer's intention.

All three examples show the weakness inherent in the word *not*. Consciously or unconsciously, the reader is dissatisfied with being told only what is not; he wishes to be told what is. Therefore, as a rule, it is better to express even a negative in positive form.

✗ **Weak**	☺ **Strong**
not honest	dishonest
not important	trifling
Did not remember	forgot
Did not pay attention to	ignored
Did not have much confidence in	distrusted

The antithesis of negative and positive is strong, and in writing, we can express the essence of this in:

☺ Not charity, but simple justice.

☺ Not that I loved Caesar less, but Rome more.

Negative words other than *not* are usually strong:

☺ The sun never sets upon the British flag.

Rule 12. Use definite, specific, concrete language.

Prefer the specific to the general, the definite to the vague, the concrete to the abstract.

✗ A period of unfavorable weather set in.

☺ It rained every day for a week.

✗ He showed satisfaction as he took possession of his well-earned reward.

☺ He grinned as he pocketed the coin.

✗ There is a general agreement among those who have enjoyed the experience that surf-riding is productive of great exhilaration.

☺ All who have tried surf-riding agree that it is most exhilarating.

If those who have studied the art of writing are in accord on any one point, it is on this: The surest method of arousing and holding the reader's attention is by being specific, definite, and concrete. Critics have pointed out how much of the effectiveness of great writers such as Homer, Dante, and Shakespeare results from their constant definiteness and concreteness. Browning, another great author, gives the reader many striking examples. Take, for instance, the lines from *My Last Duchess*:

Sir, 'twas all one! My favor at her breast,

The dropping of the daylight in the west,

The bough of cherries some officious fool

Broke in the orchard for her, the white mule

She rode with round the terrace—all and each

Would draw from her alike the approving speech,

Or blush, at least,

and those which end the poem,

Notice Neptune, though,

Taming a sea-horse, thought a rarity,

Which Claus of Innsbruck cast in bronze for me.

These words evoke vivid mental pictures. Recall how in *The Bishop Orders his Tomb in St. Praxed's Church* "the Renaissance spirit—its worldliness, inconsistency, pride, hypocrisy, ignorance of itself, love of art, of luxury, of good Latin," to quote Ruskin's comment on the poem, is made manifest in specific details and in concrete terms.

Prose, in particular narrative and descriptive prose, is made vivid by the same means. If the experiences of Jim Hawkins and of David Balfour, of Kim, of Nostromo, have seemed for the moment real to countless readers, if in reading Carlyle we have almost the sense of being physically present at the taking of the Bastille, it is because of the definiteness of the details and the concreteness of the terms used. It is not that every detail is given—that would be impossible and would serve no purpose; but that all the significant details are given, and not vaguely, but with such definiteness that the reader, in imagination, can project himself into the scene.

In exposition and in argument, you must likewise never lose your hold upon the concrete. Even when you are dealing with general principles, you must give particular instances of their application.

"This superiority of specific expressions is clearly due to the effort required to translate words into thoughts. As we do not think in generals, but in particulars—as whenever any class of things is referred to, we represent it to ourselves by calling to mind individual members of it, it follows that when an abstract word is used, the listener or reader has to choose, from his stock of images, one or more by which he may figure to himself the genus mentioned. In doing this, some delay must arise, some force be expended; and if by employing a specific term an appropriate image can be at once suggested, an economy is achieved, and a more vivid impression produced."

Herbert Spencer, from whose *Philosophy of Style* the preceding paragraph is quoted, illustrates the principle by the sentences:

> "In proportion as the manners, customs, and amusements of a nation are cruel and barbarous, the regulations of their penal code will be severe."

> "In proportion as men delight in battles, bull-fights, and combats of gladiators, will they punish by hanging, burning, and the rack."

Rule 13. Omit needless words.

Vigorous writing is concise. A sentence should contain no unnecessary words, a paragraph no unnecessary sentences, for the same reason that a drawing should have no unnecessary lines and a machine no unnecessary parts. This requires not that the writer make all his sentences short, or that he avoid all detail and treat his subjects only in outline, but that he make every word tell.

Many expressions in common use violate this principle:

✗ **Word clutter**	☺ **Concise form**
the question as to whether	whether (the question whether)
there is no doubt but that	no doubt (doubtless)
used for fuel purposes	used for fuel
he is a man who	he
in a hasty manner	hastily
this is a subject which	this subject
His story is a strange one.	His story is strange.

In particular, the expression *the fact that* should be deleted from every sentence in which it occurs.

✗ **Word clutter**	☺ **Concise form**
owing to the fact that	since (because)
in spite of the fact that	though (although)
call your attention to the fact that	remind you (notify you)
I was unaware of the fact that	I was unaware that (did not know
the fact that he had not succeeded	his failure
the fact that I had arrived	my arrival

See also under *case, character, nature,* and *system* in Chapter 5.

Who is, which was, and the like are often superfluous and should be written out of sentences.

> ✗ His brother, who is a member of the same firm

> ☺ His brother, a member of the same firm

> ✗ Trafalgar, which was Nelson's last battle

> ☺ Trafalgar, Nelson's last battle

Just as positive statement is more concise than negative, and active voice is more concise than the passive, many of the examples given under Rules 11 and 12 illustrate this principle as well.

A common violation of conciseness is the presentation of a single complex idea, step by step, in a series of sentences or independent clauses that might be more effectively combined into one.

> ✗ Macbeth was very ambitious. This led him to wish to become king of Scotland. The witches told him that this wish of his would come true. The king of Scotland at this time was Duncan. Encouraged by his wife, Macbeth murdered Duncan. He was thus enabled to succeed Duncan as king. (51 words.)

> ☺ Encouraged by his wife, Macbeth achieved his ambition and realized the prediction of the witches by murdering Duncan and becoming king of Scotland in his place. (26 words.)

> ✗ There were several less important courses, but these were the most important, and although they

did not come every day, they came often enough to keep you in such a state of mind that you never knew what your next move would be. (43 words.)

☺ These, the most important courses of all, came, if not daily, at least often enough to keep one under constant strain. (21 words.)

Rule 14. Avoid a succession of loose sentences.

This rule refers especially to loose sentences of a particular type—those consisting of two co-ordinate clauses, the second introduced by a conjunction or relative. Although single sentences of this type may be acceptable (see Rule 4), a series soon becomes monotonous and tedious. An unskilled writer will sometimes construct a whole paragraph of such sentences, using as connectives *and, but, so,* and less frequently *who, which, when, where,* and *while,* these last in non-restrictive senses (see Rule 3).

> The third concert of the subscription series was given last evening, and a large audience was in attendance. Mr. Edward Appleton was the soloist, and the Boston Symphony Orchestra furnished the instrumental music. The former showed himself to be an artist of the first rank, while the latter proved itself fully deserving of its high reputation. The interest aroused by the series has been very gratifying to the Committee, and it is planned to give a similar series annually hereafter. The fourth concert will be given on Tuesday, May 10, when an equally entertaining program will be presented.

Apart from the trite and empty nature of the above paragraph, it is weak because of the structure of its sentences, with their mechanical symmetry and sing-song. Contrast with them the sentences in the paragraphs quoted under Rule 9, or in any piece of good English prose, as the preface (Before the Curtain) to *Vanity Fair*.

If you find that you have written a series of sentences of the type described, you should recast enough of them to remove the monotony. Replace them with simple sentences, sentences of two clauses joined by a semicolon, by periodic sentences of two clauses, by sentences, loose or periodic, of three clauses—whichever best represent the real relations of the thought.

Rule 15. Express co-ordinate ideas in similar form.

This principle, that of parallel construction, requires that expressions of similar content and function should be outwardly similar. The likeness of form enables the reader to recognize more readily the likeness of content and function. The novice writer often violates this principle from a mistaken belief that he should constantly vary the form of his expressions. It is true that in repeating a statement in order to emphasize it, it may be desirable to vary its form. For illustration, see the paragraph from Stevenson quoted under Rule 9. But apart from this, the writer should follow the principle of parallel construction.

> ✗ Formerly, science was taught by the textbook method, while now the laboratory method is employed.

> ☺ Formerly, science was taught by the textbook method; now it is taught by the laboratory method.

The first version gives the impression that the writer is undecided or timid; he seems unable or afraid to choose one form of expression and hold to it. The second version shows that the writer has at least decided on the point he wants to make, and he makes it.

By this principle, an article or a preposition that applies to all the members of a series must either be used only before the first term or else be repeated before each term. In the following sentences, the first of the pair is missing an article, and the second of each is correctly written.

✗ The French, the Italians, Spanish, and Portuguese

☺ The French, the Italians, the Spanish, and the Portuguese

✗ In spring, summer, or in winter

☺ In spring, summer, or winter (In spring, in summer, or in winter)

Correlative expressions (*both, and*; *not, but*; *not only, but also*; *either, or*; *first, second, third*; and the like) should be followed by the same grammatical construction, that is, virtually, by the same part of speech. (Such combinations as "both Henry and I," "not silk, but a cheap substitute," are obviously within the rule.) Many violations of this rule (as the three below) arise from faulty arrangement; others (as the fourth example) from the use of unlike constructions.

✗ It was both a long ceremony and very tedious.

☺ The ceremony was both long and tedious.

✗ A time not for words, but action.

☺ A time not for words, but for action.

✗ Either you must grant his request or incur his ill will.

☺ You must either grant his request or incur his ill will.

✗ My objections are, first, the injustice of the measure; second, that it is unconstitutional.

☺ My objections are, first, that the measure is unjust; second, that it is unconstitutional.

See also the third example under Rule 12 and the last under Rule 13.

What if you need to express a very large number of similar ideas, say twenty? Must you write twenty consecutive sentences of the same pattern? On closer examination, you will probably find that the difficulty is imaginary, that your twenty ideas can be classified in groups, and that you need apply the principle only within each group. Otherwise, it is best to avoid difficulty by putting your statements in the form of a table.

Rule 16. Keep related words together.

The position of words in a sentence is the principal means of showing their relationship. You must therefore try to bring together the words, and groups of words, that are related in thought, and keep apart those which are not so related.

The subject of a sentence and the principal verb should not, as a rule, be separated by a phrase or clause that can be written at the beginning.

✗ Wordsworth, in the fifth book of *The Excursion*, gives a minute description of this church.

☺ In the fifth book of *The Excursion*, Wordsworth gives a minute description of this church.

✗ Cast iron, when treated in a Bessemer converter, is changed into steel.

☺ By treatment in a Bessemer converter, cast iron is changed into steel.

The objection is that the interposed phrase or clause needlessly interrupts the natural order of the main clause. Usually, however, this objection does not hold when the order is interrupted only by a relative clause or by an expression in apposition. Nor does it hold in periodic sentences in which the interruption is a deliberately used means of creating suspense (see examples under Rule 18).

Usually, the relative pronoun should come immediately after its antecedent. Note, too, that in almost every instance, starting a sentence with "There is" or any similar form of the expression should be avoided.

✗ There was a look in his eye that boded mischief.

☺ In his eye was a look that boded mischief.

✗ He wrote three articles about his adventures in Spain, which were published in *Harper's Magazine.*

☺ He published in *Harper's Magazine* three articles about his adventures in Spain.

✗ This is a portrait of Benjamin Harrison, grandson of William Henry Harrison, who became President in 1889.

☺ This is a portrait of Benjamin Harrison, grandson of William Henry Harrison. He became President in 1889.

A noun in apposition may come between antecedent and relative, because in such a combination no real ambiguity can arise.

> The Duke of York, his brother, who was regarded with hostility by the Whigs

Modifiers should come, if possible, next to the word they modify. If several expressions modify the same word, they should be so arranged to avoid ambiguity or confusing the reader.

✗ All the members were not present.

☺ Not all the members were present.

✗ He only found two mistakes.

☺ He found only two mistakes.

✗ Major R. E. Joyce will give a lecture on Tuesday evening in Bailey Hall, to which the public is invited, on "My Experiences in Mesopotamia" at eight P. M.

☺ On Tuesday at eight P. M., Major R. E. Joyce will give in Bailey Hall a lecture on "My Experiences in Mesopotamia." The public is invited.

Rule 17. In summaries, keep to one tense.

In summarizing the action of a drama, you should always use the present tense. In summarizing a poem, story, or novel, you should preferably use the present, though you may use the past if you prefer. If the summary is in the present tense, antecedent action should be expressed by the perfect; if in the past, by the past perfect.

> An unforeseen chance prevents Friar John from delivering Friar Lawrence's letter to Romeo. Meanwhile, owing to her father's arbitrary change of the day set for her wedding, Juliet has been compelled to drink the potion on Tuesday night, with the result that Balthasar informs Romeo of her supposed death before Friar Lawrence learns of the non-delivery of the letter.

But whichever tense is used in the summary, a past tense in indirect discourse or in indirect question should remain unchanged.

> The Friar confesses that it was he who married them.

Apart from the exceptions noted, whichever tense you choose, you should use throughout. Shifting from one tense to the other gives the appearance of uncertainty and lack of clarity (compare Rule 15).

In presenting the statements or the thought of someone else, as in summarizing an essay or reporting a speech, you should avoid intercalating such expressions as "he said," "he stated," "the speaker added," "the speaker then went on to say," "the author also thinks," and the like. Indicate clearly right from the start that what follows is summary, and then waste no words in repeating the notification.

In newspapers and in many kinds of textbooks, summaries of one kind or another may be indispensable, and it is a useful exercise for children in primary schools to retell a story in their own words. But in the criticism or interpretation of literature, you should be careful to avoid dropping into summary. You may find it necessary to devote one or two sentences to indicating the subject, or the opening situation, of the work you are discussing; you may cite numerous details to illustrate its qualities. But you should aim to write an orderly discussion supported by evidence, not a summary with occasional comment. Similarly, if the scope of your discussion includes a number of works, you will as a rule do better not to take them up singly in chronological order but to aim from the beginning at establishing general conclusions.

Rule 18. Place the emphatic words of a sentence at the end.

The proper place in a sentence for the word, or group of words, which you want to make most prominent is usually the end.

> ✗ Humanity has hardly advanced in fortitude since that time, though it has advanced in many other ways.

> ☺ Humanity, since that time, has advanced in many other ways, but it has hardly advanced in fortitude.

> ✗ This steel is principally used for making razors, because of its hardness.

> ☺ Because of its hardness, this steel is principally used in making razors.

The word or group of words entitled to this position of prominence is usually the logical predicate, that is, the *new* element in the sentence, as it is in the second example.

The effectiveness of the periodic sentence arises from the prominence which it gives to the main statement.

> Four centuries ago, Christopher Columbus, one of the Italian mariners whom the decline of their own republics had put at the service of the world and of adventure, seeking for Spain a westward passage to the Indies as a set-off against the achievements of Portuguese discoverers, lighted on America.

> With these hopes and in this belief I would urge you, laying aside all hindrance, thrusting away all private aims, to devote yourself unswervingly and unflinchingly to the vigorous and successful prosecution of this war.

The other prominent position in the sentence is the beginning. Any element in the sentence, other than the subject, may become emphatic when placed first.

> Deceit or treachery he could never forgive.

> So vast and rude, fretted by the action of nearly three thousand years, the fragments of this architecture may often seem, at first sight, like works of nature.

A subject written first in its sentence may be emphatic, but hardly by its position alone. In this sentence,

> Great kings worshipped at his shrine,

the emphasis upon *kings* arises largely from its meaning and from the context. To receive special emphasis, the subject of a sentence must take the position of the predicate.

Through the middle of the valley flowed a winding stream.

The principle that the proper place for what is to be made most prominent is the end applies equally to the words of a sentence, to the sentences of a paragraph, and to the paragraphs of a composition.

Chapter 4

A FEW MATTERS OF FORM

Headings. Leave a blank line after the title or heading of a manuscript. On succeeding pages, begin typing on the first line.

Numerals. Do not spell out dates or serial numbers. Write them in figures or in Roman notation, as may be appropriate.

> August 9, 1918 (9 August 1918)
>
> Rule 3
>
> Chapter XII
>
> 352nd Infantry

Parentheses. A sentence containing an expression in parenthesis is punctuated, outside of the marks of parenthesis, exactly as if the expression in parenthesis were absent. The expression within is punctuated as if it stood by itself, except that the final stop is omitted unless it is a question mark or an exclamation point.

> I went to his house yesterday (my third attempt to see him), but he had left town.
>
> He declares (and why should we doubt his good faith?) that he is now certain of success.

Note that when a wholly detached expression or sentence is parenthesized, such as this example, the final stop is written before the last mark of parenthesis.

Quotations. Formal quotations, cited as documentary evidence, are introduced by a colon and enclosed in quotation marks.

> The provision of the Constitution is: "No tax or duty shall be laid on articles exported from any state."

Quotations grammatically in apposition or the direct objects of verbs are preceded by a comma and enclosed in quotation marks.

> I recall the maxim of La Rochefoucauld, "Gratitude is a lively sense of benefits to come."
>
> Aristotle says, "Art is an imitation of nature."

Quotations of an entire line (or more) of verse, are begun on a fresh line and centered, but need not be enclosed in quotation marks.

> Wordsworth's enthusiasm for the Revolution was at first unbounded:
>
> > Bliss was it in that dawn to be alive,
> >
> > But to be young was very heaven!

Quotations introduced by *that* are regarded as indirect discourse and are not be enclosed in quotation marks.

> Keats declares that beauty is truth, truth beauty.

Proverbial expressions and familiar phrases of literary origin require no quotation marks.

These are the times that try men's souls.

He lives far from the madding crowd.

The same is true of colloquialisms and slang.

References. In scholarly work requiring exact references, abbreviate titles that occur frequently, giving the full forms in an alphabetical list at the end. As a general practice, give the references in parenthesis or in footnotes, not in the body of the sentence. Omit the words *act, scene, line, book, page, volume,* except when referring to only one of them. Punctuate as indicated below.

> In the second scene of the third act

> In III.ii (still better, simply insert III.ii in parenthesis at the proper place in the sentence)

> After the killing of Polonius, Hamlet is placed under guard (IV.ii. 14).

> *2 Samuel* i:17–27

> *Othello* II.iii. 264–267, III.iii. 155–161.

Hyphenation. If room exists at the end of a line for one or more syllables of a word but not for the whole word, divide the word, unless this involves cutting off only a single letter, or cutting off only two letters of a long word.

[*Editor's Note:* As with some other rules outlined in the original *Elements of Style,* writing practices change over time, and this applies to the rules of hyphenation. Most modern writing guides advise against hyphenating words of any length if fewer than three letters would remain on the current line or the subsequent line. Thus, the rules below, which recommend, for example, hyphenating "treat-ed" may not apply to your own writing. Refer to your style guide for instructions on how to handle hyphenation correctly.]

No hard and fast rule for all words exists, but the most frequently cited principles are:

1. Divide the word according to its formation:

    know-ledge (not knowl-edge); Shake-speare (not Shakes-peare); de-scribe (not des-cribe); atmo-sphere (not atmos-phere).

2. Divide "on the vowel:"

    edi-ble (not ed-ible); propo-sition; ordi-nary; reli-gious; oppo-nents; regu-lar; classi-fi-ca-tion (three divisions allowable); deco-rative; presi-dent.

3. Divide between double letters, unless they come at the end of the simple form of the word:

    Apen-nines; Cincin-nati; refer-ring; but tell-ing.

Do not divide before final -*ed* if the *e* is silent:

treat-ed (but not roam-ed or nam-ed).

The proper handling of consonants in combination is best illustrated by examples:

for-tune; pic-ture; sin-gle; presump-tuous; illus-tration; sub-stan-tial (either division); indus-try; instruc-tion; sug-ges-tion; incen-diary.

Titles. For the titles of literary works, scholarly usage prefers italics with capitalized initials. Style rules followed by editors and publishers vary, some using italics with capitalized initials, others using Roman with capitalized initials and with or without quotation marks. As a rule of thumb, use italics, except in writing for a periodical or in accordance with a style guide that follows a different practice. Omit the initial *A* or *The* from titles when you place the possessive before them.

> The *Iliad*; the *Odyssey*; *As You Like It*; *To a Skylark*; *The Newcomes*; *A Tale of Two Cities*

> But Dickens's *Tale of Two Cities*.

Chapter 5

WORDS AND EXPRESSIONS OFTEN MISUSED

Some of the forms here listed, as *like I did*, are downright bad English; others, as the split infinitive, have their defenders, but are in general disfavor and therefore inadvisable to use; still others, as *case, factor, feature, interesting, one of the most*, are good in their place, but are constantly obtruding themselves into places where their use is ill-advised. If you will make it your purpose from the beginning to express accurately your own individual thought, and you'll refuse to be satisfied with a ready-made formula that saves you the trouble of doing so, this last set of expressions will cause you little trouble. But if you find that in a careless moment you have used one of them, you should probably not patch up the sentence by substituting one word or set of words for another but recast it completely, as illustrated in a number of examples below and in others under Rules 12 and 12.

[*Editor's Note:* At the time Strunk's *Elements of Style* was published in the early 1900s, split infinitives were regarded as bad English by grammarians, and writers were cautioned to avoid these forms. Today, however, they are commonplace and accepted in the major style guides endorsed by editors and publishers. For example, *Chicago Manual of Style* advises: "Sometimes it is perfectly acceptable to split an infinitive verb with an adverb to add emphasis or to produce a natural sound." For further details on split infinitives and other contemporary grammar rules, refer to *Elements of Style 2017.*]

All right. Idiomatic in familiar speech as a detached phrase in the sense, "Agreed," or "Go ahead." In other uses better avoided. Always written as two words. "Alright" is commonly used in informal writing, but it is not a word and should not appear in an edited manuscript.

As good or better than. Expressions of this type should be corrected by rearranging the sentence.

> ✗ My opinion is as good or better than his.

> ☺ My opinion is as good as his, or better (if not better).

> ☺ My opinion is as good as his, if not better.

As to whether. *Whether* is sufficient; see Rule 13.

Bid. Takes the infinitive without *to*. The past tense in the sense "ordered" is *bade*.

But. Unnecessary after *doubt* and *help*.

> ✗ I have no doubt but that

> ☺ I have no doubt that

> ✗ He could not help see but that

> ☺ He could not help seeing that

The overuse of *but* as a conjunction leads to the fault discussed under Rule 14. A loose sentence formed with *but* can always be converted into a periodic sentence formed with *although,* as illustrated under Rule 4.

Particularly awkward is the following of one *but* by another, making a contrast to a contrast or a reservation to a reservation. This is easily corrected by re-arrangement.

> ✗ America had vast resources, but she seemed almost wholly unprepared for war. But within a year she had created an army of four million men.

> ☺ America seemed almost wholly unprepared for war, but she had vast resources. Within a year she had created an army of four million men.

Can. Means *am (is, are) able*. Do not use as a substitute for *may*.

Case. The *Concise Oxford Dictionary* begins its definition of this word: "instance of a thing's occurring; usual state of affairs." In these two senses, the word is usually unnecessary.

> ✗ In many cases, the rooms were poorly ventilated.

> ☺ Many of the rooms were poorly ventilated.

> ✗ It has rarely been the case that any mistake has been made.

> ☺ Few mistakes have been made.

See Wood, *Suggestions to Authors*, pp. 68–71, and Quiller-Couch, *The Art of Writing*, pp. 103–106.

Certainly. Used indiscriminately by some writers, much as others use *very*, to intensify any and every statement. A mannerism of this kind, bad in speech, is even worse in writing.

Character. Often simply redundant, used from a mere habit of wordiness.

✗ Acts of a hostile character

☺ Hostile acts

Claim, vb. With object-noun, means *lay claim to*. May be used with a dependent clause if this sense is clearly involved: "He claimed that he was the sole surviving heir." (But even here, "claimed to be" would be better.) Not to be used as a substitute for *declare, maintain,* or *charge*.

Clever. This word has been greatly overused; it is best restricted to ingenuity displayed in small matters.

Compare. To *compare to* is to point out or imply resemblances between objects regarded as essentially of different order; to *compare with* is mainly to point out differences between objects regarded as essentially of the same order. Thus life has been compared to a pilgrimage, to a drama, to a battle; the U.S. Congress may be compared with the British Parliament. Paris has been compared to ancient Athens; it may be compared with modern London.

Consider. Not followed by *as* when it means "believe to be." "I consider him thoroughly competent." Compare, "The lecturer considered Cromwell first as soldier and second as administrator," where "considered" means "examined" or "discussed."

Data. A plural, like *phenomena* and *strata*.

☺ These data were tabulated.

[*Editor's Note:* Today, the word "data" commonly is used as a reference to either singular or plural. This rule from the original *Elements of Style* is now obsolete.]

Dependable. A needless substitute for *reliable, trustworthy*.

Different than. Not permissible. Substitute *different from, other than,* or *unlike*.

Divided into. Not to be misused for *composed of*. The line is sometimes difficult to draw: plays are divided into acts, but poems are composed of stanzas.

Don't. Contraction of *do not*. The contraction of *does not* is *doesn't*.

Due to. Incorrectly used for *through, because of,* or *owing to* in adverbial phrases:

✗ He lost the first game, due to carelessness.

In correct use related as predicate or as modifier to a particular noun:

☺ This invention is due to Edison.

☺ losses due to preventable fires

Folk. A collective noun, equivalent to *people*. Use the singular form only.

Effect. As a noun, the word means *result*; as a verb, it means to *bring about, accomplish* (not to be confused with *affect*, which means "to influence").

As a noun, often loosely used in perfunctory writing about fashion, music, painting, and other arts: "an Oriental effect;" "effects in pale green;" "very delicate effects;" "broad effects;" "subtle effects;" "a charming effect was produced by." The writer who has a definite meaning to express will not resort to such vague phrasing.

Etc. Equivalent to *and the rest, and so forth,* and not to be used if one of these would be insufficient, that is, if the reader would be left in doubt as to any important particulars. Least open to objection when it represents the last terms of a list already given in full, or immaterial words at the end of a quotation.

At the end of a list introduced by *such as, for example,* or any similar expression, *etc.* is incorrect.

Fact. Use this word only for matters capable of direct verification, not matters of judgment. That a certain event happened on a given date, and that lead melts at a certain temperature, are facts. But such conclusions as that Napoleon was the greatest of modern generals, or that the climate of California is delightful, however incontestable they may be, are not properly facts.

For the expression *the fact that,* see Rule 13.

Factor. A hackneyed word; the expressions of which it forms part can usually be replaced by something more direct and idiomatic.

> ✗ His superior training was the great factor in his winning the match.

> ☺ He won the match by being better trained.

> ✗ Heavy artillery has become an increasingly important factor in deciding battles.

> ☺ Heavy artillery has played a constantly larger part in deciding battles.

Feature. Another hackneyed word; like *factor* it usually adds nothing to the sentence in which it occurs.

✗ A feature of the entertainment especially worthy of mention was the singing of Miss A.

(It is better to use the same number of words to tell what Miss A. sang, or if the program has already been given, to tell how she sang.)

As a verb, in the advertising sense of *offer as a special attraction*, it should be avoided.

Fix. Colloquial in America for *arrange, prepare, mend*. In technical and other formal writing, restrict it to its literary senses: *fasten, make firm or immovable*, etc.

Get. The colloquial *have got* for *have* should not be used in writing. The preferable form of the participle is *got*.

He is a man who. A common type of redundant expression; see Rule 13.

✗ He is a man who is very ambitious.

☺ He is very ambitious.

✗ Spain is a country which I have always wanted to visit.

☺ I have always wanted to visit Spain.

However. In the meaning *nevertheless*, this word should not be used first in its sentence or clause.

✗ The roads were almost impassable. However, we at last succeeded in reaching camp.

☺ The roads were almost impassable. At last, however, we succeeded in reaching camp.

When *however* is written first, it means in whatever way or to whatever extent.

> ☺ However you advise him, he will probably do as he thinks best.

> ☺ However discouraging the prospect, he never lost heart.

Interesting. Avoid this word as a perfunctory means of introduction. Instead of announcing that what you are about to tell is interesting, make it so.

> ✗ An interesting story is told of

> ☺ (Tell the story without preamble.)

> ✗ In connection with the anticipated visit of Mr. B. to America, it is interesting to recall that he

> ☺ Mr. B., who it is expected will soon visit America

Kind of. Not to be used as a substitute for *rather* (before adjectives and verbs), or except in familiar style, for *something like* (before nouns). Restrict it to its literal sense: "Amber is a kind of fossil resin;" "I dislike that kind of notoriety." The same holds true of *sort of.*

Less. Should not be misused for *fewer*.

> ✗ He had less men than in the previous campaign

> ☺ He had fewer men than in the previous campaign

Less refers to quantity, *fewer* to number. "His troubles are less than mine" means "His troubles are not so great as mine." "His troubles are fewer than mine" means "His troubles are not so numerous as mine." It is, however, correct to say, "The signers of the petition were less than a hundred," where the round number *a hundred* is something like a collective noun, and *less* is thought of as meaning a less quantity or amount.

Like. Do not misuse for *as*. *Like* governs nouns and pronouns; before phrases and clauses, the equivalent word is *as*.

✗ We spent the evening like in the old days.

☺ We spent the evening as in the old days.

✗ He thought like I did.

☺ He thought as I did (like me).

Line, along these lines. *Line* in the sense of *course of procedure*, conduct, *thought*, is allowable, but has been so much overworked, particularly in the phrase *along these lines*, that a writer who aims at freshness or originality should discard it entirely.

✗ Mr. B. also spoke along the same lines.

☺ Mr. B. also spoke, to the same effect.

✗ He is studying along the line of French literature.

☺ He is studying French literature.

Literal, literally. Often incorrectly used in support of exaggeration or violent metaphor.

✗ A literal flood of abuse.

☺ A flood of abuse.

✗ Literally dead with fatigue

☺ Almost dead with fatigue (dead tired)

Lose out. Meant to be more emphatic than *lose*, but actually less so because of its commonness. The same holds true of *try out, win out, sign up*. With numerous verbs, *out* and *up* form idiomatic combinations: *find out, run out, cheer up, dry up, make up*, and others, each distinguishable in meaning from the simple verb. *Lose out* is not.

Most. Not to be used for *almost*.

✗ Most everybody

☺ Almost everybody

✗ Most all the time

☺ Almost all the time

Nature. Often simply redundant, used like *character*.

✗ Acts of a hostile nature

☺ Hostile acts

Often vaguely used in such expressions as a "lover of nature;" "poems about nature." Unless more specific statements follow, the reader cannot tell whether the poems have to do with natural scenery, rural life, the sunset, the untracked wilderness, or the habits of squirrels.

Near by. Adverbial phrase, not yet fully accepted as good English, though the analogy of *close by* and *hard by* seems to justify it. *Near*, or *near at hand*, is as good, if not better.

Not to be used as an adjective; use *neighboring*.

Oftentimes, ofttimes. Archaic forms, no longer in good use. Substitute the word *often* instead.

One hundred and **one.** Retain the *and* in this and similar expressions.

One of the most. Avoid beginning essays or paragraphs with this construction, as, "One of the most interesting developments of modern science is," etc. "Switzerland is one of the most interesting countries of Europe." There is nothing wrong in this; it is simply threadbare and overused.

A common blunder is to use a singular verb in a relative clause following this or a similar expression, when the relative is the subject.

> ✗ One of the ablest men that has attacked this problem.

> ☺ One of the ablest men that have attacked this problem.

Participle for verbal noun.
In the first sentences of the next two examples, *asking* and *accepting* are used as present participles; in the second examples, they are verbal nouns (gerunds). The construction shown in the first sentences is occasionally found and has its defenders. Yet it is easy to see that the second examples have to do not with a prospect of the Senate, but with a prospect of accepting. Here, at least, the construction is plainly illogical.

> ✗ Do you mind me asking a question?

> ☺ Do you mind my asking a question?

✗ There was little prospect of the Senate accepting even this compromise.

☺ There was little prospect of the Senate's accepting even this compromise.

As the authors of *The King's English* point out, there are sentences apparently, but not really, of this type, in which the possessive is not appropriate. For instance:

✗ I cannot imagine Lincoln refusing his assent to this measure.

In this sentence, what the writer cannot imagine is Lincoln himself, in the act of refusing his assent. Yet the meaning would be virtually the same, except for a slight loss of vividness, if he had written:

☺ I cannot imagine Lincoln's refusing his assent to this measure.

By using the possessive, the writer will always be on the safe side.

In the examples above, the subject of the action is a single, unmodified term, immediately preceding the verbal noun, and the construction is as good as any that could be used. But any sentence in which the wording is clumsy, or in which the use of the possessive is awkward or impossible, should be recast.

✗ In the event of a reconsideration of the whole matter's becoming necessary

☺ If it should become necessary to reconsider the whole matter

✗ There was great dissatisfaction with the decision of the arbitrators being favorable to the company.

☺ There was great dissatisfaction that the arbitrators should have decided in favor of the company.

People. *The people* is a political term, not to be confused with *the public*. From the people comes political support or opposition; from the public comes artistic appreciation or commercial patronage.

Possess. Do not use as a mere substitute for *have* or *own*.

✗ He possessed great courage.

☺ He had great courage (was very brave).

✗ He was the fortunate possessor of

☺ He owned

Prove. The past participle is *proved*.

Respective, respectively. These words may usually be omitted from sentences without altering the meaning.

✗ Works of fiction are listed under the names of their respective authors.

☺ Works of fiction are listed under the names of their authors.

✗ The one mile and two mile runs were won by Jones and Cummings respectively.

☺ The one mile and two mile runs were won by Jones and by Cummings.

In some kinds of formal writing, as geometrical proofs, it may be appropriate to use *respectively*, but it should not appear in everyday writing.

Shall, Will. The future tense requires *shall* for the first person, will for the second and third. The formula to express the speaker's belief regarding his future action or state is *I shall*; *I will* expresses his determination or his consent.

[*Editor's Note:* Today, *shall* is rarely used, except in legal writing. *Chicago Manual of Style* states that it is only used to mean "has a duty to," and *shall not* is never used as the negative.]

Should. See under *Would*.

So. Avoid, in writing, the use of *so* as an intensifier: "so good;" "so warm;" "so delightful." On the use of *so* to introduce clauses, see Rule 4.

Sort of. See under *Kind of*.

Split Infinitive. There is precedent from the fourteenth century downward for interposing an adverb between *to* and the infinitive which it governs, but the construction is in disfavor and is avoided by nearly all careful writers.

    ✗ To diligently inquire

    ☺ To inquire diligently

[*Editor's Note:* In modern writing, split infinitives are used fairly often and deemed permissible by most of the major style guides. See the opening of Chapter 5 for additional remarks on the use of split infinitives.]

State. Not to be used as a mere substitute for *say, remark* Restrict it to the sense of *express fully or clearly*, as, "He refused to state his objections."

Student Body. A needless and awkward expression meaning no more than the simple word *students*.

    ✗ A member of the student body

    ☺ A student

    ✗ Popular with the student body

    ☺ Liked by the students

    ✗ The student body passed resolutions.

    ☺ The students passed resolutions.

System. Often used without need; most of the time, such use is unnecessary and creates word clutter.

    ✗ Dayton has adopted the commission system of government.

    ☺ Dayton has adopted government by commission.

    ✗ The dormitory system

    ☺ Dormitories

Thanking You in Advance. This sounds as if the writer meant, "It will not be worth my while to write to you again." In making your request, write, "Will you please," or "I will appreciate," and if anything further seems necessary, write a letter of acknowledgment later.

They. A common grammatical error is the use of the plural pronoun when the antecedent is a distributive expression such as *each, each* one, *everybody, everyone, many a man,* which, though implying more than one person, requires the pronoun to be in the singular. Similar to this, but with even less justification, is the use of the plural pronoun with the antecedent *anybody, anyone, somebody, someone,* the intention being to avoid the awkward "he or she," or to avoid committing oneself to either. Some writers who are unsure of the correct construction will even write, "A friend of mine told me that they," etc.

Use *he* with all the above words, unless the antecedent is or must be feminine.

[*Editor's Note:* This is another of the numerous grammar rules which have changed over time. Today, the practice of writing *he* unless the feminine is indicated has fallen out of favor, giving way to other practices, including clumsy attempts at substitution. For a detailed discussion on gender issues in grammar, see *Elements of Style 2017*, Chapter 6 (Nouns—People, Places, Things), and Chapter 7 (Getting Personal With Pronouns).]

Very. Use this word sparingly. Where emphasis is necessary, use words that are strong rather than relying on the overused *very.*

Viewpoint. Do not misuse this, as many do, for *view* or *opinion.* Instead, write *point of view.*

While. Avoid the indiscriminate use of this word in place of *and, but,* and *although.* Many writers use it frequently as a substitute for *and* or *but,* either from a desire to vary the connective or from uncertainty which of the two connectives is the more appropriate. In this use, it is best replaced by a semicolon.

> ✗ The office and salesrooms are on the ground floor, while the rest of the building is devoted to manufacturing.

> ☺ The office and salesrooms are on the ground floor; the rest of the building is devoted to manufacturing.

Its use as a virtual equivalent of *although* is allowable in sentences where no ambiguity or absurdity is created.

> ☺ While I admire his energy, I wish it were employed in a better cause.

This is entirely correct, as shown by the paraphrase,

> I admire his energy; at the same time, I wish it were employed in a better cause.

Compare:

> ✗ While the temperature reaches 95 degrees in the daytime, the nights are often chilly.

> ☺ Although the temperature reaches 95 degrees in the daytime, the nights are often chilly.

The paraphrase,

> The temperature reaches 95 degrees in the daytime; at the same time the nights are often chilly,

shows why the use of *while* is incorrect.

In general, the writer will do well to use *while* only with strict literalness, in the sense of *during the time that*.

Whom. Often incorrectly used for *who* before *he said* or similar expressions, when it is really the subject of a following verb.

✗ His brother, whom he said would send him the money

☺ His brother, who he said would send him the money

✗ The man whom he thought was his friend

☺ The man who (that) he thought was his friend (whom he thought his friend)

Worthwhile. Overworked as a term of vague approval and (with *not*) of disapproval. Strictly applicable only to actions: "Is it worthwhile to study grammar?"

✗ His books are not worthwhile.

☺ His books are not worth reading (are not worth his while to read; are worthless).

The use of *worthwhile* before a noun ("a worthwhile story") is faulty grammar and should be avoided in writing.

Would. A conditional statement in first person requires *should*, not *would*.

I should not have succeeded without his help.

The equivalent of *shall* in indirect quotation after a verb in the past tense is *should*, not *would*.

He predicted that before long we should have a great surprise.

[*Editor's Note:* Because *shall* is less prevalent today, the rule calling for *should* to be used in conditional first person statements may not apply, depending on the sentence and its intended meaning. For instance, if the writer wishes to convey that something ought to happen or should have happened, he might write, "She should have known better," and "She should have turned left." Otherwise, *would* is often used today in conditional first person statements.]

To express habitual or repeated action, the past tense, without *would*, is usually sufficient, and from its brevity, more emphatic.

✗ Once a year he would visit the old mansion.

☺ Once a year he visited the old mansion.

Chapter 6

SPELLING

The spelling of English words is not fixed and invariable, nor does it depend on any other authority than general agreement. In this day and age, agreement as to the spelling of most words is practically unanimous. At any given moment, however, a relatively small number of words may be spelled in more than one way. As one of these forms comes to be generally preferred, the less customary form comes to look obsolete and is discarded. From time to time new forms, mostly simplifications, are introduced by innovators, and either win their place or die of neglect.

The practical objection to unaccepted and over-simplified spellings is the disfavor with which they are received by the reader. They distract his attention and exhaust his patience. He reads the form *though* automatically, without giving it a second thought; he reads the abbreviation *tho* and must mentally supply the missing letters, diverting a fraction of his attention from what is being read. The writer has defeated his own purpose.

[*Editor's Note:* In the first edition of Strunk's *Elements of Style*, this chapter supplied a list of sixty-five commonly misspelled words. As the English language has expanded over the past century, new words have been introduced into everyday vocabulary which cause writers headaches and embarrassing typos. Accordingly, we have expanded the original list to the following 171 entries.

WORDS OFTEN MISSPELLED

absence	acceptable
accidentally	accommodate
acquire	acquit
address	advice
affect	all right
amateur	apparent
arctic	argument
atheist	beginning
believe	bellwether
benefit	bicycle
broccoli	bureau
calendar	camaraderie
category	ceiling
cemetery	challenge
changeable	coarse
collectible	column
committed	conscience
conscientious	consensus
course	criticize
daiquiri	decease
deceive	definite
descent	describe
desperate	despise
develop	disappoint

disastrous	discipline
dissipate	drunkenness
duel	dumbbell
ecstasy	effect
embarrass	equipment
exercise	exhilarate
existence	experience
fascinate	February
fiery	fluorescent
foreign	formerly
gauge	grateful
guarantee	harass
height	hierarchy
humorous	hypocrisy
ignorance	immediate
immediately	impostor
incident	incidentally
independent	indispensable
inoculate	intelligence
jealous	jewelry
judgment	knowledge
latter	led
leisure	liaison
license	lose
maintenance	maneuver
marriage	mathematics
medieval	mediocre

memento	millennium
miniature	minuscule
miscellaneous	mischief
mischievous	misspell
murmur	mysterious
necessary	neighbor
noticeable	nuclear
occasion(ally)	occurred
occurrence	odyssey
opportunity	parallel
perseverance	personnel
piece	pigeon
playwright	possession
precede	preceding
prejudice	principal/principle
privilege	pronunciation
publicly	pursue
questionnaire	raspberry
receive	recommend
referred	repetition
restaurant	rhyme
rhythm	ridiculous
sacrilegious	schedule
scissors	seize
separate	sergeant
shepherd	siege
similar	simile

special	supersede
there/their/they're	thorough
threshold	through
tragedy	twelfth
tyranny	undoubtedly
vacuum	villain
weather	Wednesday
weird	

Note that a single consonant (other than *v*) preceded by a stressed short vowel is doubled before -*ed* and -ing: *planned, letting, beginning.* (*Coming* is an exception.)

Write *to-day, to-night, to-morrow* (but not *together*) with a hyphen.

Write *any one, every one, some one, some time* (except in the sense of *formerly*) as two words.

[*Editor's Note:* The last two rules are obsolete. Present-day writers use the unhyphenated forms of *today, tonight* and *tomorrow,* and in most cases, omit the spaces from the pronouns *anyone, everyone, someone,* and from *sometime.* In some sentences, however, the two-word forms would still be used. For instance: "Any one of those men could be the thief," and "I have read every one of Stephen King's books." Likewise, *some time* written as two words denotes a passage of time, as, "Some time has passed since we met," or "I will spend some time visiting you when I come to Ireland."]

Chapter 7

EXERCISES ON CHAPTERS II AND III

1. Punctuate:

In 1788 the King's advisers warned him that the nation was facing bankruptcy therefore he summoned a body called the States-General believing that it would authorize him to levy new taxes. The people of France however were suffering from burdensome taxation oppressive social injustice and acute scarcity of food and their representatives refused to consider projects of taxation until social and economic reforms should be granted. The King who did not realize the gravity of the situation tried to overawe them collecting soldiers in and about Versailles where the sessions were being held. The people of Paris seeing the danger organized militia companies to defend their representatives. In order to supply themselves with arms they attacked the Invalides and the Bastille which contained the principal supplies of arms and munitions in Paris.

On his first continental tour begun in 1809 Byron visited Portugal Spain Albania Greece and Turkey. Of this tour he composed a poetical journal Childe Harold's Pilgrimage in which he ascribed his experiences and reflections not to himself but to a fictitious character Childe Harold described as a melancholy young nobleman prematurely familiar with evil sated with pleasures and embittered against humanity. The substantial merits of the work however lay not in this shadowy and somewhat theatrical figure but in Byron's spirited descriptions of wild or picturesque scenes and in his eloquent championing of Spain and Greece against their oppressors. On his return to England in 1811 he was persuaded rather against his own judgment into allowing the work to be published. Its success was almost unprecedented in his own words he awoke and found himself famous.

2. Explain the difference in meaning:

'God save thee, ancyent Marinere!
'From the fiends that plague thee thus—

Lyrical Ballads, 1798

'God save thee, ancient Mariner!
From the fiends, that plague thee thus!—

Lyrical Ballads, 1800

3. Explain and correct the errors in punctuation:

This course is intended for Freshmen, who in the opinion of the Department are not qualified for military drill.

A restaurant, not a cafeteria where good meals are served at popular prices.—*Advt.*

The poets of *The Nation*, for all their intensity of patriotic feeling, followed the English rather than the Celtic tradition, their work has a political rather than a literary value and bears little upon the development of modern Irish verse.

We were in one of the strangest places imaginable. A long and narrow passage overhung on either side by a stipendous barrier of black and threatening rocks.

Only a few years ago after a snow storm in the passes not far north of Jerusalem no less than twenty-six Russian pilgrims perished amidst the snow. One cannot help thinking largely because they made little attempt to save themselves.

4. Identify and correct the faults in the following sentences:

During childhood his mother had died.

Any language study is good mind training while acquiring vocabulary.

My farm consisted of about twenty acres of excellent land, having given a hundred pounds for my predecessor's lease.

Prepared to encounter a woman of disordered mind, the appearance presented by Mrs. Taylor at his entrance greatly astonished him.

Pale and swooning, with two broken legs, they carried him into the house.

Count Cassini, the Russian plenipotentiary, had several long and intimate conversations during the tedious weeks of the conference with his British colleague, Sir Arthur Nicholson.

But though they had been victorious in the land engagements, they were so little decisive as to lead to no important results.

Knowing nothing of the rules of the college or of its customs, it was with the greatest difficulty that the Dean could make me comprehend wherein my wrong-doing lay.

Fire, therefore, was the first object of my search. Happily, some embers were found upon the hearth, together with potato-stalks and dry chips. Of these, with much difficulty,

I kindled a fire, by which some warmth was imparted to our shivering limbs.

In this connection a great deal of historic fact is introduced into the novel about the past history of the cathedral and of Spain.

Over the whole scene hung the haze of twilight that is so peaceful.

Compared with Italy, living is more expensive.

It is a fundamental principle of law to believe a man innocent until he is proved guilty, and once proved guilty, to remain so until proved to the contrary.

Not only had the writer entrée to the titled families of Italy in whose villas she was hospitably entertained, but by royalty also.

It is not a strange sight to catch a glimpse of deer along the shore.

Earnings from other sources are of such a favorable character as to enable a splendid showing to be made by the company.

But while earnings have mounted amazingly, the status of affairs is such as to make it impossible to predict the course events may take, with any degree of accuracy.

-The End-

ELEMENTS OF STYLE
STUDY GUIDE

Study Guide

The original *Elements of Style* was written a century ago by William Strunk Jr., an English professor at Cornell University. Over the years, it has been reprinted in various editions, and today, it is widely regarded as a grammar classic. Despite the fact that some of the grammar rules in the book are now out of date, it is required reading for many students taking composition and other writing classes.

This particular version, entitled *Elements of Style: Classic Edition*, remains true to Prof. Strunk's original work and contains all of the material published in the first edition, presented in the same sequence. The following revisions and additions to the book have been made:

The editor of this Classic Edition, has inserted brief notations throughout the book, identifying grammar and style rules that have become obsolete over the years. Rather than revising the original text, notes have been added where appropriate and are labeled "*Editor's Note:*".

The editor has added a Foreword, described below. Also, the typography for the e-book version has been restyled for optimum display on modern Kindle devices and other e-book readers; and the paperback edition has been restyled to give the book a clean, modern appearance. Blank, lined pages are included in the back of the book, which readers can use to jot down grammar-related notes.

A new Study Guide has been added (what you are now reading); and as part of the restyling in both the e-book and print editions, recognizable symbols have been added to examples so that readers can differentiate at a glance between correctly written grammar examples and errors.

Foreword

An eight-page overview of grammar and style and its relevance today is presented in the Foreword, entitled, *Grammar and Style for the 21st Century*. This is new material that does not appear in the original *Elements of Style*. It is excerpted from *Elements of Style 2017*, edited by Richard De A'Morelli, with revisions appropriate to introduce readers to Prof. Strunk's grammar handbook. Of particular interest are passages that explain: why a working knowledge of grammar and style is important to students of English, and to all writers, today; the role that style guides serve in writing and editing; and the fact that major style guides sometimes give conflicting advice. Examples are given to show why adhering to a consistent style throughout a manuscript is important; and discussion on the term "point of view" provides a refresher on the meaning of first, second, and third person in grammar.

Chapter 1

This first chapter of Prof. Strunk's book runs two pages and contains introductory remarks by the author. It opens with a paragraph defining the primary aims of this grammar book. The professor then acknowledges individuals who contributed to the preparation of his manuscript.

Prof. Strunk provides a suggested reading list that includes grammar and composition books popular around the time the first edition of *Elements of Style* was published, and the chapter concludes with a reminder that writers must learn the rules of grammar before they can break them or venture into unorthodox styles.

Chapter 2

In this chapter, Prof. Strunk introduces the first seven rules in a series under the chapter head, *Elementary Rules of Usage*. In summary, these rules are:

Rule 1 discusses guidelines on how to form the possessive singular of nouns by adding 's, and notable exceptions to this rule.

Rule 2 examines how to correctly punctuate (with commas) sentences having three or more elements and a single conjunction. An editorial notation is included here advising that this particular method of punctuation makes use of what is called the serial comma, or Oxford comma.

Rule 3 focuses on the rules for enclosing parenthetic expressions between commas.

Rule 4 is another comma-related guideline which states that this mark of punctuation must be placed before a conjunction introducing a co-ordinate clause.

In Rule 5, the writer is cautioned against using a comma to join independent clauses.

In Rule 6, Prof. Strunk explains that sentences should not be split into. He gives examples of how this can create unacceptable sentence fragments.

Rule 7 advises that a participial phrase at the beginning of a sentence must refer to the grammatical subject. Strunk offers various examples of how this rule should be applied.

Chapter 3

Additional grammar rules are presented in Chapter 3, under the heading *Elementary Principles of Composition*.

The numbering resumes at Rule 8, which focuses on the importance of the paragraph as the principal unit of composition. Rule 9 points out that each paragraph must begin with a topic sentence. Several pages of discussion on this point follow, with clear examples of how to develop paragraphs for a typical academic composition.

Rule 10 covers active voice and why it is often advisable to use it. Prof. Strunk also mentions situations where using the passive voice is appropriate.

Rule 11 examines the importance of putting statements in positive form. Doing so allows the writer to make definite, forceful assertions. Numerous examples are given showing how overuse of the word *not* can lead to weak and indecisive writing.

Rule 12 builds on the preceding advice and explores the advantages of using definite, specific, concrete language. Nearly three pages are devoted to this crucial topic.

The next, Rule 13, advises that vigorous writing is concise. The writer must endeavor to omit needless words from sentences, and unnecessary sentences from paragraphs. This rule addresses the problem of "word clutter" raised by many present-day grammar teachers and writing instructors.

Rule 14 offers helpful guidance on how to achieve concise, crisp prose by avoiding the habit of writing loose structures that can become monotonous to readers. Strunk explains that one fix for this is to avoid repetitive use of connectives such as *and, but,* and *so* in typical paragraphs.

Rule 15 builds on the preceding advice, exploring the principle of parallel construction and giving examples of preferable writing styles, as well as sentence structures to be avoided.

Rule 16 addresses the concern that related words should be kept together to avoid interrupting the flow of the main clause. Prof. Strunk explains how the subject of a sentence and its verb should not usually be separated by a phrase or clause that can written at the beginning of the sentence with better effect. He also explains how this rule applies to nouns, pronouns, and modifiers.

In Rule 17, the writer is cautioned to avoid changing tenses when summarizing actions or facts. Examples are given that show how violating this principle can lead to stilted or ambiguous writing.

The final rule, Rule 18, explains that the emphatic words of a sentence should be placed at the end for maximum effect.

Chapter 4

This chapter, entitled *A Few Matters of Form*, offers a set of brief instructions on how to write: headings, numerals, references, titles; and hyphenation is discussed. An editor's notation appears here, alerting readers to the fact that the rules for hyphenation have changed over the years, and an updated rule is given.

This chapter also discusses how to handle parentheses as well as quotations in typical sentences. These sections are brief and give the writer only a bit of insight into how these topics should be handled.

Chapter 5

This chapter offers a list of words and expressions that are often misused. The list is alphabetized and begins with an entry for *alright*, which Prof. Strunk explains in not a word and should never appear in an edited manuscript. It concludes with entries on the always vexing *Whom*," the over-used word *worthwhile*, and an entry on the use of *would* versus *should*. This final entry includes an editor's note that addresses present-day usage of these expressions, which has changed over the years. Prof. Strunk's admonition to avoid split infinitives also is addressed in a separate note from the editor that explains split infinitives are acceptable today in most forms of writing.

Chapter 6

A list of frequently misspelled words in the English language is presented in Chapter 6. Prof. Strunk featured sixty-five words on his list in the first edition, and the list in this Classic Edition has been expanded to 171 words that give modern writers headaches.

Chapter 7

This final chapter in the book offers a set of exercises on Chapters 2 and 3 which were included in Prof. Strunk's *Elements of Style*. These exercises are of limited benefit because the answers were not provided in the book.

Study Guide

This study guide follows Chapter 7. It did not appear in previous editions and has been added by the current editor in the thought that a brief overview may prove helpful to students who are required to study this grammar book.

-#-

Elements of Style 2017
Edited by Richard De A'Morelli
(Nonfiction Reference/Writing)

Elements of Style 2017 presents a collection of grammar, style, and punctuation rules to help you to write well, self-edit efficiently, and produce a grammar-perfect final draft. It is a major update to William Strunk's classic 1921 grammar book. Much has changed in the world since then—some of the rules in Strunk's book are obsolete, and many new grammar and style rules have come into play that writers must know.

Bestselling author/editor Richard De A'Morelli shares his 30+ years of experience as a senior editor and explains what you need to know about grammar and style in a clear and simple way. Written in plain English, with easy-to-follow examples, this book takes the headache out of great writing. Read any chapter, follow the practical advice, and you will see an overnight improvement in your writing. Read a chapter a day, and in just a few weeks, you will be amazed by the polished quality of your final draft.

If you write anything at all for work, school, or your own enjoyment, you should have a copy of this writer's handbook on your desk. Learn how to improve your grammar and polish your writing to perfection with *Elements of Style 2017*.

Buy online or visit: http://vu.org/books/elements

ISBN Numbers	Editions
978-1-988236-26-1	MOBI/Kindle
978-1-988236-28-5	Paperback
978-1-088236-31-5	Paperback Large Print

Live Well. Be Happy.

by Richard De A'Morelli

(Inspirational/Self-Help)

This book is about your life and your search for happiness. It will help you to realize that you can change your life by changing how you think and react to the world around you. You will learn steps you can take to stay sane and balanced in a crazy world. And you'll discover how making simple changes in your daily routine can help you find your path to happiness.

In these pages, you will learn that happiness in life depends on the choices you make, staying positive, and never giving up on your hopes and dreams. You'll discover simple ways to reduce stress, overcome depression, build confidence, and conquer unhealthy habits. You will also learn how to stay balanced and maintain your peace of mind using natural techniques such as deep relaxation, visualization, rhythm breathing, and meditation.

This inspiring book reminds us that life is short, and we must make the most of the precious time we are given. If you've been looking for a book that will encourage you to change your life and give you a helping hand to move forward, this short course in modern living may be that inspiration. The book also makes a wonderful gift for someone in need of encouragement and a step-by-step approach to getting their life on a positive track.

Buy online or visit: http://vu.org/books/live-well

978-1-988234-09-3	MOBI/Kindle
978-1-988234-08-6	EPUB Digital
978-1-988234-04-8	Paperback
978-1-988234-04-9	Paperback Large Print
978-1-988236-47-6	Hardcover

As A Man Thinks
Edited by Richard De A'Morelli
(Inspirational/Self-Help)

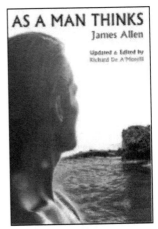

This special edition of James Allen's classic book *As a Man Thinketh* explores how the power of thought affects you on every level, and how you can take control of your life and destiny. The way you think creates every condition in your life, good and bad. If you have been beset by disappointment and failure, the empowering wisdom in this book can change your life. You will learn how to use the power of your mind to build confidence, unlock hidden talents, cope with depression and stress, overcome habits, and achieve health and vitality. Learn how to use these timeless insights to build a bright future and become the master of your destiny.

This edition retains the flavor of James Allen's practical advice but the book has been updated to a modern style that is easy to follow and enjoyable to read. Also, the book has been expanded—each chapter includes additional insights, explanations, and points to remember that can empower you to change your life by changing the way you think.

Buy online or visit: http://vu.org/books/as-a-man-thinks

978-1-988236-08-7	MOBI/Kindle
978-1-988236-09-4	EPUB Digital
978-1-988236-10-0	Paperback
978-1-988236-11-7	Paperback Large Print
978-1-988236-12-4	Hardcover Edition

Apocalypse Orphan
By Tim Allen
(Science Fiction-Fantasy)

Commander Orlando Iron Wolf is aboard the International Space Station when a blinking light on his computer console alerts him to a fast moving comet headed for a collision with planet Earth.

With no way to stop the impending doomsday, the world descends into panic and anarchy. Massive transport ships are built to colonize the moon, and evacuation of a chosen few begins.

After a shuttle mission to study the approaching comet goes awry, Wolf is forced into cryogenic deep sleep, and the on-board computer assumes control of the ship.

Wolf awakens 50,000 years later to a wildly different earth. Endowed with incredible strength, he finds himself caught in a war between primitive tribes, and his survival depends on Syn, an advanced computer intelligence who has fallen in love with him.

Will Wolf be able to help restore Earth to its past glory or is civilization doomed to fail?

Buy online or visit: http://vu.org/books/ao

ISBN Numbers	Editions
978-1-988236-00-1	MOBI/Kindle
978-1-988236-07-0	EPUB Digital
978-1-988236-01-8	Paperback
978-1-088236-02-5	Paperback Large Print
978-1-988236-03-2	Hardcover Edition

Notes

Notes

Notes

Notes

Notes

Notes

Made in the USA
San Bernardino, CA
22 May 2018